Places We Live

Living Beside the
Sea

Ellen Labrecque

raintree

Raintree is an imprint of Capstone Global Library Limited, a company incorporated in England and Wales having its registered office at 7 Pilgrim Street, London, EC4V 6LB – Registered company number: 6695582

www.raintree.co.uk
myorders@raintree.co.uk

Edited by James Benefield and Brenda Haugen
Designed by Richard Parker
Original illustrations © Capstone Global Library Ltd
Picture research by Jo Miller
Production by Helen McCreath
Originated by Capstone Global Library Ltd
Printed and bound in China

ISBN 978 1 406 28776 9 (hardback)
18 17 16 15 14
10 9 8 7 6 5 4 3 2 1

ISBN 978 1 406 28783 7 (paperback)
19 18 17 16 15
10 9 8 7 6 5 4 3 2 1

British Library Cataloguing in Publication Data
A full catalogue record for this book is available from the British Library.

Acknowledgments
We would like to thank the following for permission to reproduce the following photographs: Alamy: Bjarki Reyr MR, 20, Geof Kirby, 12, JB-2078, 8, Mark Conlin, 21, USA, 11; Dreamstime: Thomas Perkins, 5; Newscom: Getty Images/AFP/Gregory Boissy, 23, Hindustan Times, 27, Michael Weber Image Broker, 17, Robert Harding/Purcell-Holmes, 22, Robert Harding/Tony Waltham, 16, Steve Smith Stock Connection Worldwide, 14, ZUMA Press/Koichiri Tezuka-Mainichi Shimbun, 15; Shutterstock: gary yim, 25, Marek Stefunko, 19, nui7711, 26, oksana perkins, 7, Paul J Martin, 10, Razvy, 9, spirit of america, 18, trubavin, 4, WAMVD, cover, wdeon, 24; Superstock: age fotostock/Martin Zwick, 13.

We would like to thank Rachel Bowles for her invaluable help in the preparation of this book.

Contents

What is the sea? 4

Where is the sea? 6

Living by the sea 8

Living by the sea in the past 10

City living by the sea 12

Wild weather 14

Safe from the sea? 16

Getting around 18

What is school like? 20

Where do people work? 22

Fun things to do 24

Living by the sea in the future 26

Fun facts 28

Quiz 29

Glossary 30

Find out more 31

Index 32

Some words are shown in bold, **like this**. You can find out what they mean by looking in the glossary.

What is the sea?

Seas are giant areas of salty water. The biggest seas are called oceans. They are one of the most important places people find food. They also provide **minerals**, oil and natural gas from their seabeds.

Some beaches are flat and sandy.

Some beaches can have lots of rocks and pebbles on them. You can still have fun there, though!

The sea is home to a huge number of plants and animals, even more than live on dry land. It's a good place for people to live, too. The sea absorbs the Sun's heat, so that people and the whole planet don't get too hot.

Where is the sea?

Oceans and seas cover over 70 per cent of the world's surface. The world's seas don't really have borders. Water flows between them. But we have different names for different parts of the sea.

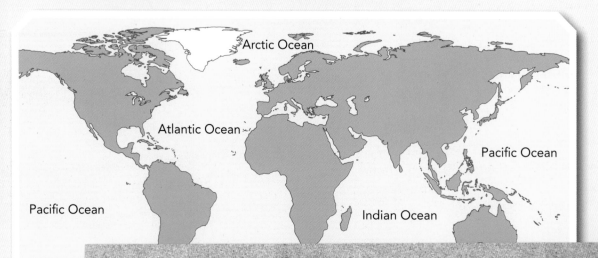

Arctic Ocean

Atlantic Ocean

Pacific Ocean

Pacific Ocean

Indian Ocean

Earth's major oceans listed by size

1. Pacific Ocean, 165 million square kilometres (about 64 million square miles)

2. Atlantic Ocean, 106,460,000 square kilometres (about 41 million square miles)

3. Indian Ocean, 73,440,000 square kilometres (about 28 million square miles)

Over 4.5 million people live in Sydney, Australia, a city on the Pacific Ocean.

The Pacific Ocean is the biggest ocean on Earth. It covers one-third of the world's surface. It stretches from Antarctica almost up to the Arctic Circle. Many people around the world live near the Pacific Ocean.

Living by the sea

People all over the world live in **settlements** by the sea. Some people live in these homes all year around. Other people own homes here, but live and work inland.

The sea is a place to both live and relax.

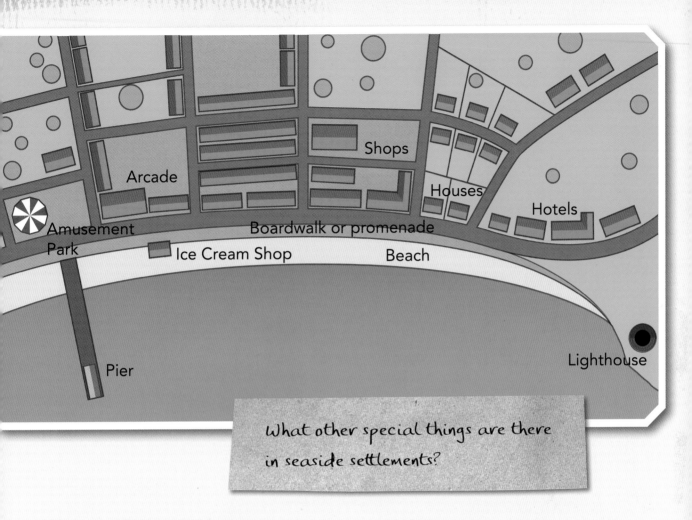

Shops

Arcade

Houses

Hotels

Amusement Park

Boardwalk or promenade

Ice Cream Shop

Beach

Lighthouse

Pier

What other special things are there in seaside settlements?

Seaside settlements have many things other types of settlements have. For example, they have shops and houses. But they also might have special things, such as a lighthouse. This is a tall building with a large light that warns ships that there are nearby rocks.

Living by the sea in the past

Fishing **communities** have always lived by the sea. But only rich people went on holiday there. Poor people didn't have enough money to travel to the seaside. This all changed when railways were built in the 1800s.

Trains made travelling to the beach much cheaper.

In 1870, a boardwalk was built in Atlantic City, New Jersey, USA.

As more people came to the sea, the area became built up. Many more homes, shops and restaurants were built. People can walk along the **piers, promenades** and **boardwalks**. Promenades can also be part of seawalls.

City living by the sea

Many people live in cities by the sea. Cities grew up here as the sea helped people **trade** with distant countries. By the sea they could easily sail in and out with the things they were trading.

Cape Town, South Africa, has a busy **port**. The city is where the Atlantic and Indian oceans meet.

Aberdeen, Scotland sits on the North Sea where a lot of oil drilling takes place.

Some cities have grown up by the sea because of oil. Most people who work on **oil rigs** live by the sea. People on rigs help dig for oil that is far below the sea and deep into the seabed.

Wild weather

Living by the sea can be dangerous. During storms, the sea can flood the land and can destroy buildings and hurt people. Some towns have built beach houses on stilts to protect the houses from flooding.

Seawalls are built to stop water from flooding settlements.

Tsunami waters can be up to 30 metres (100 feet) high.

Tsunamis are especially dangerous. They are a series of waves that send lots of water onto the land. Underwater earthquakes can cause them. A tsunami hit Japan in 2011 killing as many as 18,000 people.

Getting around

You can get to most seaside places by road. **Tourists** travel on cruise ships to see different seaside towns. People even cruise to the coasts of Antarctica, even though there are no towns there!

Antarctica has no seaside towns but plenty of penguins!

The Bajau live in raised houses or on boats.

The Bajau people in Southeast Asia, on the Pacific Ocean don't just travel on boats. Some live in house boats. Others live in stilt houses. They say when they spend a night on land they feel land sick, not seasick.

Where do people work?

People can have regular jobs such as doctors and teachers and live by the sea. However, there are jobs found just here. There are fishermen, coastguards and beach lifeguards.

Coastguards protect people in boats out at sea. Lifeguards keep people safe at the beach.

Laird Hamilton lives in Hawaii, USA, and surfs waves that are 30 metres (100 feet) high.

Some people who live in beach towns work in jobs that serve **tourists**. For example, they work in hotels or restaurants. Some people who live in beach towns surf for a living.

Fun things to do

Some people love to visit the seaside. They can swim, explore the water and play on the beach. People sunbathe and play sport on most kinds of beaches. If the beach is sandy, people can build sand castles.

Volleyball is a great beach sport.

Peggy's Cove in Nova Scotia, Canada, is a great rocky beach to explore. You can find lots of things in rock pools.

If you like adventure, rocky beaches offer great places to explore. If it's too rocky, you can get in a boat. You could search for wildlife, from dolphins to sea turtles, that are swimming in the waters.

Living by the sea in the future

Some scientists believe living by the sea is getting harder because of **climate change**. Sea levels are rising as ice and **glaciers** melt. This could cause flooding, which can destroy seaside homes. There is also water **pollution**.

Water pollution kills plant and animal life.

In some places, people go on organized beach litter picking.

Work is being done to clean up the seas. In some places, rules have been set to stop people from dumping rubbish into the sea. Groups such as Save Our Seas help to teach people how to protect seas and seaside homes.

Fun facts

- People who study oceans are called oceanographers.

- Nearly 2.4 billion people in the world live within 100 kilometres (60 miles) of the sea.

- World Oceans Day is celebrated every year on 8 June.

- The largest animal in the ocean is the blue whale.

- During the wintertime, the Arctic Ocean is almost completely covered in sea ice.

- Some studies tell us that people who live by the sea are happier than those who live inland!

Quiz

Which of the following sentences are true? Which are false?

1. There is more land than water on Earth.

2. The biggest ocean in the world is the Arctic.

3. Underwater earthquakes can cause tsunamis.

4. Erosion is not dangerous.

5. Sea levels are going down.

5. False. Some scientists think that levels are rising because of climate change.

4. False. Erosion can destroy people's homes.

3. True.

2. False. The world's biggest ocean is the Pacific.

1. False. The oceans and seas cover about 72 per cent of the Earth's surface.

Glossary

boardwalk wooden walkway by the sea, across sand, where people like to stroll

climate change change in weather patterns or the planet's temperature over many years

community group of people or animals who share the same things, such as where they live

erosion when land or rock has been worn or ground down over time by water, ice, snow or wind

glacier huge river of ice or iceberg. You can find these near and in the Arctic or the Antarctic.

mineral special substance from rocks, that can be found in the sea, for example salt

oil rig large, raised platform out in the sea. People work on these to drill oil from below the seabed.

pier raised walkway from land out over water

pollution when harmful substances are released into the sea, air or ground. This can hurt or kill animals, plants and even people.

port where boats load or unload what they carry

promenade walkway along a the seaside

settlement place where people live, such as a village, town or city

tide regular rise and fall of the height of the sea

tourist person who visits another place for fun

trade when you buy or sell things

Find out more

Books

100 Things You Should Know About the Seashore,
  Steve Parker (Mason Crest Publishers, 2010)

Beachcombing: Exploring the Seashore,
  Jim Arnosky (Puffin, 2014)

Living by the Seaside: Our Local Area, Richard Spilsbury
  (Raintree, 2010)

Websites

www.nhm.ac.uk/nature-online/earth/oceans/index.html

Learn more about what you can find in the sea on this
Natural History Museum website.

http://saveourseas.com
Learn what you can do to help protect and save our
seas at this website.

http://worldoceansday.org
Celebrate our seas and seaside living when you visit
this website.

Index

animals 25, 28
Antarctica 18
Arctic Ocean 28
Atlantic Ocean 6, 12

beaches 9, 14, 16,
  17, 22, 24, 25
blue whales 28
boardwalks 11

cities 7, 8, 12–13
cliffs 9
climate change 26
coastguards 22
coasts 9, 16
cruises 18

dolphins 25

earthquakes 15
erosion 16, 17

fishing communities
10
flooding 14, 26
fun, having 24–25

homes 8, 9, 11,
  14, 19
house boats 19

ice, sea 26, 28
Indian Ocean 6, 12
isolated communities
  20

lifeguards 22
living by the sea
  8, 26, 27

North Sea 13

oceanographers 28
oceans 4, 6, 7
oil 4, 13

Pacific Ocean 6, 7
piers 11
pollution 26
ports 12

salty water 4
schools 20–21
sea levels 26

seawalls 14
sports 24
stilt houses 14, 19
surfing 23

tourism 18, 23
travel 10, 18–19
tsunamis 15
turtles 25

work 13, 22–23